WELCOME TO
FELICITY'S WORLD ❧ 1774
Growing Up in Colonial America

THE AMERICAN GIRLS COLLECTION

American Girl

Printed in Singapore.
00 01 02 03 04 05 TWP 10 9 8 7 6 5 4
The American Girls Collection®, the American Girl logo, Felicity®, and
Felicity Merriman® are trademarks of Pleasant Company.

Written by Catherine Gourley
Edited by Camela Decaire and Jodi Evert
Historical and Editorial Consulting by American Historical Publications
Designed and Art Directed by Mengwan Lin and Jane S. Varda
Cover Illustration by Dan Andreasen
Interior Illustrations by David Henderson, Laszlo Kubinyi, Susan McAliley, and Susan Moore
Researched by Mary Davison, Sally Jacobs, and Sally Wood
Prop Research and Styling by Jean doPico
Photography by Jamie Young

Library of Congress Cataloging-in-Publication Data
Welcome to Felicity's world, 1774 / [written by Catherine Gourley; edited by Camela Decaire and Jodi Evert;
designed by Mengwan Lin and Jane S. Varda; photography by Jamie Young].
p. cm.
Summary: Provides an in-depth look at daily life and historical events in the American colonies
during the Revolutionary War, including home life, work, medicine, and play.
ISBN 1-56247-768-4
1. United States—Social life and customs—To 1775—Juvenile literature.
2. United States—Social life and customs—1775–1783—Juvenile literature.
[1. United States—Social life and customs—To 1775. 2. United States—Social life and customs—1775–1783.
3. United States—History—Revolution, 1775–1783.]
I. Gourley, Catherine, 1950–   II. Young, Jamie, ill. III. Pleasant Company Publications.
E163.W45 1999 98-47025 973.2—dc21 CIP AC

Table of Contents

Welcome to Felicity's World.....1

Chapter One   *Growing Up*.....6

Chapter Two   *At Home, at Work*.....20

Chapter Three   *Every Man (and Woman) His Own Doctor*.....34

Chapter Four   *Disturbing the King's Peace*.....42

A Peek into the Future.....58

Welcome to Felicity's World

"Haven't you heard?" asked Annabelle in a mean voice. "A few days ago in Yorktown, a mob of colonists threw chests of tea into the river. The tea was on a ship that had come from England."

"But why did they do it?" asked Felicity.

"Because they are hot-heads!" said Annabelle.

—Felicity Learns a Lesson

In 1774, rumors of war were swirling through Williamsburg like fog on a winter's morning. People in shops, taverns, and homes talked about the unfair ways the king of England treated the colonists. Patriots like Felicity's father did not think it was fair to pay taxes to the king for things like tea that they bought in America. Loyalists like Felicity's grandfather thought it was wrong for colonists to go against the king. Felicity wasn't sure what to think. The tea ceremony was an important part of her education as a gentlewoman. Should she drink tea at Miss Manderly's, or should she support the Patriots and politely refuse?

Felicity Merriman is a fictional character. But the place and the time of her story are real. In fact, all the characters in Felicity's world are based on the memories, the letters, and the diaries of real girls and women, shopkeepers and plantation owners, apprentices and slaves who lived during one of the most exciting and dangerous times in American history. Like Felicity, they too had to decide if they were American Patriots or British Loyalists.

In this book, you will travel more than two hundred years back in time and step into Felicity's world. You will meet real people who lived in the American colonies and hear their true stories. The journey begins as most journeys do . . . with a map.

The New World

Felicity was born in Virginia, one of the 13 American colonies ruled by King George III in England. By 1774, thousands of people from Europe and Africa had come to America, the New World. Some were brought against their will, while others eagerly crossed the ocean in hope of a better life.

But life in the colonies was about to turn upside down, and all because of taxes. The king wanted the colonists to pay taxes on everything from paper to paint. In England, people had the right to vote on whether they would be taxed. As English citizens, the colonists expected the same right. When the king passed still another tax—this time on tea—without letting the colonists vote, it made them so angry that some boarded a ship in Boston Harbor and dumped its whole cargo of tea overboard. Patriots called the act the Boston Tea Party. The king called it rebellion.

In crowded cities like London, homeless families roamed the streets. Children stole what they could to eat.

① ENGLAND
The only people in England who could own land were the *gentry* (JEN-tree)—those born into the upper classes. Many families sailed to America in hope of finding a different world where any colonist could buy land and build a new life.

② EUROPE
In some European countries, people who did not follow their rulers' religions might be put in prison or tortured. In America they could worship the way they wanted to.

③ KING GEORGE III
England had helped the colonies to grow and prosper. In return, King George thought the colonists should obey his rules. When they rebelled, he was furious.

ATLANTIC OCEAN

N
W · E
S

EUROPE

IRELAND · SCOTLAND · ENGLAND

① ③

FRANCE

②

SPAIN

PORTUGAL

AFRICA

⑥

⑥ AFRICA

In Africa, slave traders forced captured men, women, and children onto ships bound for America. There, thousands of slaves were needed to tend fields. The southern colonies produced huge crops of tobacco that England prized.

⑤ THE BACK COUNTRY

The wilderness lands were home to tribes of Native Americans. As colonists arrived, one chief said, "They are coming like flocks of birds to settle on the land." To him, land was like sunlight. It could not be bought or sold. To the colonists, land meant wealth and power. They wanted all they could get.

④ BOSTON BLOCKADE

King George punished the colonists for dumping his tea by sending ships to block off Boston Harbor. No ships could enter or leave. The people of Boston couldn't even fish in their own waters. They worried they might starve.

British warships surrounding a busy dock in Boston Harbor

3

The Coming Storm

The king's blockade of Boston Harbor put half of the city out of work. When news about what the king had done reached the rest of the colonies, many colonists were furious. *Delegates*, or representatives, from each of the colonies decided to meet in Philadelphia to discuss what they could do. They called their meeting the First Continental Congress. For days they argued fiercely—some wanted to break free from the king's rule, while others still wanted to try to get along with England. Delegate John Adams wrote to his wife, Abigail: *A storm is coming*. He meant war with England was possible. None of the delegates wanted war—at least not yet. First they decided to send a letter to the king demanding their rights as British citizens.

A POWERFUL NATION
In England, King George welcomed the coming storm. "Blows must decide" the fate of the colonies, he said. The king was sure that he could keep the colonies under contro After all, England had a large army and nav The colonies had no army, no navy, and no government to rule the people.

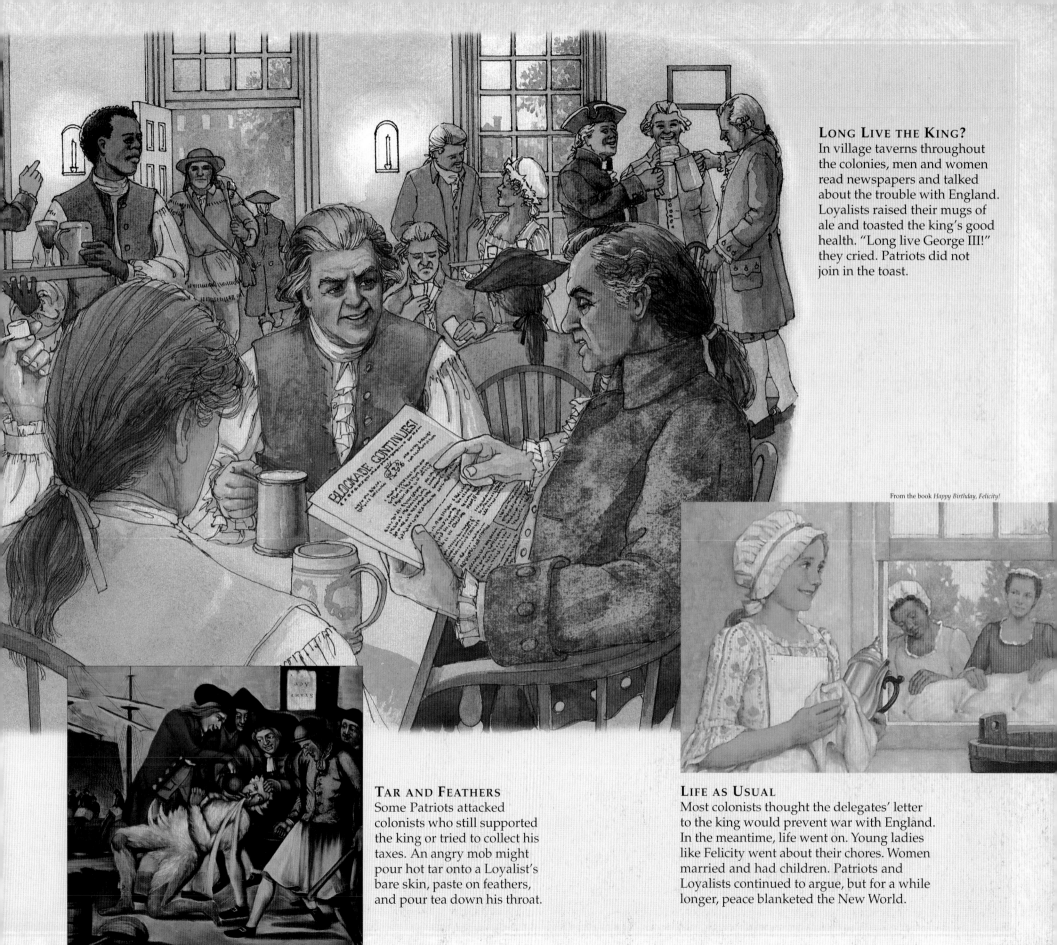

LONG LIVE THE KING?

In village taverns throughout the colonies, men and women read newspapers and talked about the trouble with England. Loyalists raised their mugs of ale and toasted the king's good health. "Long live George III!" they cried. Patriots did not join in the toast.

From the book Happy Birthday, Felicity!

TAR AND FEATHERS

Some Patriots attacked colonists who still supported the king or tried to collect his taxes. An angry mob might pour hot tar onto a Loyalist's bare skin, paste on feathers, and pour tea down his throat.

LIFE AS USUAL

Most colonists thought the delegates' letter to the king would prevent war with England. In the meantime, life went on. Young ladies like Felicity went about their chores. Women married and had children. Patriots and Loyalists continued to argue, but for a while longer, peace blanketed the New World.

Welcome Little Stranger

A family of five, like Felicity's, was rather small. Many parents had eight or more children. Families often celebrated a new baby with feasts and parties for a week or longer. Childbirth was also a time of worry. People didn't know how to prevent or treat childhood diseases that doctors can easily cure today. One new father wrote in his family Bible: *Elizabeth, born August 9, 1757. Lord do according to thy will with her.*

CHRISTENING GOWN
In well-to-do families, babies wore gowns when they were *christened*, or given a name and welcomed into the church community.

Whistle

A BABY'S BIRTH
Babies were born at home, usually with the help of a *midwife*—a woman who helps mothers during childbirth.

PIN PILLOWS
Pincushions hung on doorways to announce the birth of a baby. Handmade pins spelled out the happy news, and the pillow reminded friends not to knock loudly in case the baby was sleeping.

Some pinheads were made of glass.

WOODEN RATTLE
Baby toys often had simple designs carved into them. Look for diamonds, hearts, and a fish on this rattle.

Coral handle

BELLS AND WHISTLES
This coral baby's rattle is three toys in one—a whistle, a jingle bell rattle, and a good luck charm. Coral was a good luck symbol that was also good for teething.

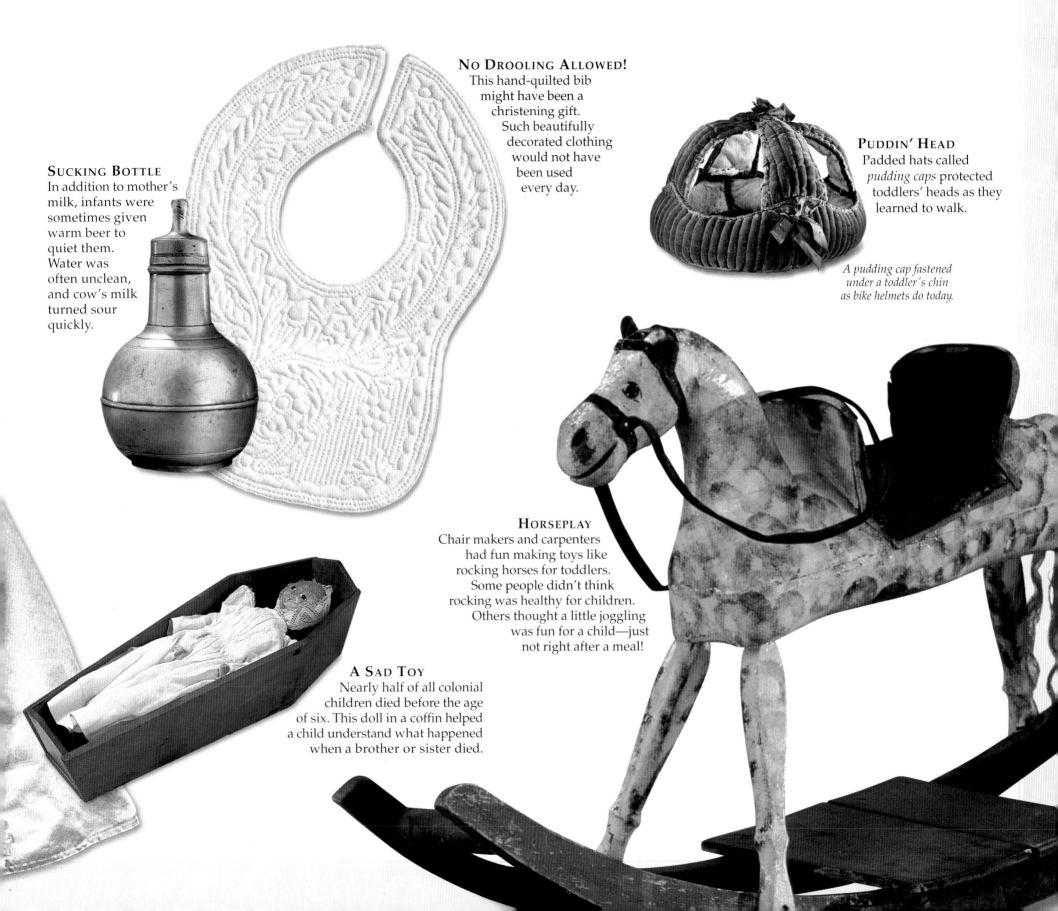

SUCKING BOTTLE
In addition to mother's milk, infants were sometimes given warm beer to quiet them. Water was often unclean, and cow's milk turned sour quickly.

NO DROOLING ALLOWED!
This hand-quilted bib might have been a christening gift. Such beautifully decorated clothing would not have been used every day.

PUDDIN' HEAD
Padded hats called *pudding caps* protected toddlers' heads as they learned to walk.

A pudding cap fastened under a toddler's chin as bike helmets do today.

HORSEPLAY
Chair makers and carpenters had fun making toys like rocking horses for toddlers. Some people didn't think rocking was healthy for children. Others thought a little joggling was fun for a child—just not right after a meal!

A SAD TOY
Nearly half of all colonial children died before the age of six. This doll in a coffin helped a child understand what happened when a brother or sister died.

Playtme

Children quickly became helpers in housework and farmwork. Even so, they found time for fun and games. Children, and even adults, flew kites and played Tag in summer. They sledded and skated in winter. And they played with toys. Most toys were handmade. With the help of a jackknife, a willow branch became a whistle. Or, with a little imagination, acorns became a tiny tea set. Other toys imported from England were treasured and passed on to younger sisters and brothers.

FASHION DOLLS

Most dolls were not playthings. *Milliners*, or the owners of clothing shops, used them to show the latest clothing fashions.

GAMES FOR ALL

Children often played the same games as their parents. Both adults and children played cards, dice, and dominoes.

GRACES

The object of this game was to throw and catch a hoop using two sticks. To catch the hoop, girls held the sticks straight. To throw the hoop, they crossed the sticks like scissors.

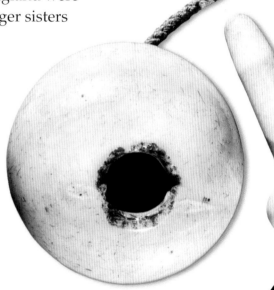

WASH-DAY GAMES

Colonial Badminton was called *Battledore and Shuttlecock*. *Battledore* comes from the Spanish word *batidor*, which means "to beat." A battledore was originally a racket-shaped tool used to stir and beat laundry during washing.

ALL-TIME FAVORITES

Colonial children played lots of games that children still play today. Blindman's Buff, Hide-and-Seek, Ring-Around-a-Rosie, and others have long been popular.

These children are playing Frog in the Middle. The seated girl, or Frog, must tag someone in the ring without leaving her seat.

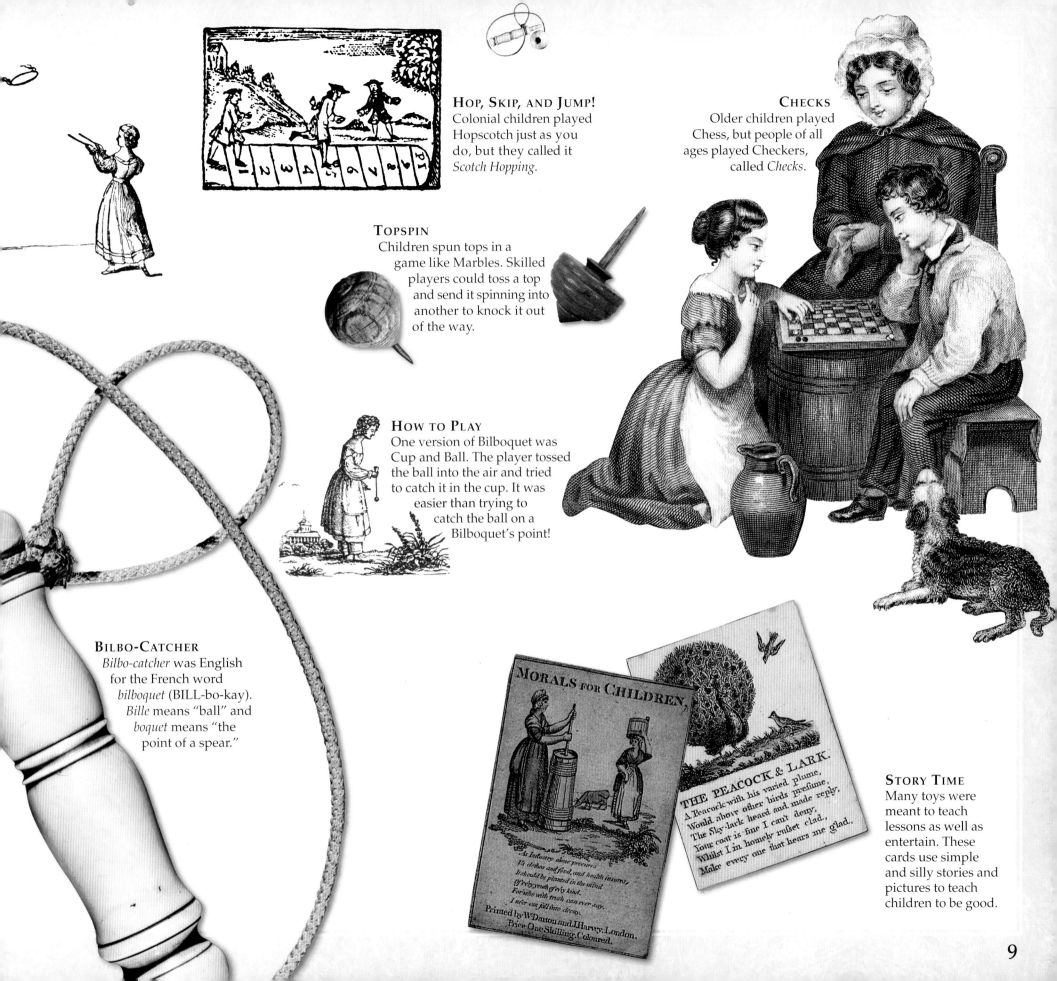

HOP, SKIP, AND JUMP!
Colonial children played Hopscotch just as you do, but they called it *Scotch Hopping*.

CHECKS
Older children played Chess, but people of all ages played Checkers, called *Checks*.

TOPSPIN
Children spun tops in a game like Marbles. Skilled players could toss a top and send it spinning into another to knock it out of the way.

HOW TO PLAY
One version of Bilboquet was Cup and Ball. The player tossed the ball into the air and tried to catch it in the cup. It was easier than trying to catch the ball on a Bilboquet's point!

BILBO-CATCHER
Bilbo-catcher was English for the French word *bilboquet* (BILL-bo-kay). *Bille* means "ball" and *boquet* means "the point of a spear."

MORALS FOR CHILDREN.

THE PEACOCK & LARK.

A Peacock with his varied plume,
Would above other birds presume,
The Sky-lark heard, and made reply,
Your coat is fine I can't deny,
Whilst I in homely ruffset clad,
Make every one that hears me glad.

STORY TIME
Many toys were meant to teach lessons as well as entertain. These cards use simple and silly stories and pictures to teach children to be good.

At School

C hildren usually learned their first letters and numbers at home, but they soon had formal lessons, too. In the northern colonies, well-to-do children often attended finishing schools. Ten-year-old Anna Green Winslow was sent to Boston to attend two schools: one for *penmanship*, or handwriting, and one for sewing. Imagine how Felicity would have felt, separated from her family! Other families hired private tutors to teach their children at home. Thomas Jefferson's daughter Patsy had a private tutor. But her father wrote in a letter how his ten-year-old daughter was to spend every hour of every day!

My Dear Patsy,
With respect to the distribution of your time, the following is what I should approve:
1. From eight to ten, practice music.
2. From ten to one, dance one day and draw another.
3. From one to two, draw on the day you dance, and write a letter the next day.
4. From three to four, read French.
5. From four to five, exercise yourself in music.
6. From five till bedtime, read English, write, and so forth.

A see-through sheet of cow's horn protected a book just as plastic does today.

HORNBOOK
A child often learned to read by using a *hornbook*, a paddle with the Lord's Prayer or the alphabet mounted on it. Children used their hornbooks to play Shuttlecock, too!

Colonists sealed their letters with melted wax. The seals were symbols of a family's or an individual's wealth. (1)

Extra ink dripped off a pen into a quill holder so a writer could reuse the ink. (2)

(3) *Ink was brewed from the juices of pressed flowers or the bark from trees and stored in inkwells.*

(4) *Girls practiced their letters— drawings, too!—in a booklet of blank pages called a* **copyboo**

PENMANSHIP
Beautiful handwriting was a sign of good education. Writing masters knew several *hands*, or styles of letters.

Anna Green
Aa Bb Cc

MUSICAL TALENT
Young ladies often learned to play the *spinet* or *harpsichord*, a small piano-like instrument.

Ten-year-old Anne Anthony stitched her whole family on her sampler, even the dog! Can you find it?

A SAMPLE OF THEIR SKILL
By the age of ten, most girls had sewn their first sampler. Then they practiced more fancy needlework. They learned to embroider, quilt, darn, and knit.

⑤ *Writers sprinkled **pounce**, a powder of ground-up bone, onto the wet ink to dry it.*

QUALITY STITCHING
A girl's qualities as a gentlewoman were judged, in part, by her sewing ability. Girls stitched pillows, handkerchiefs, and even some of their own dresses to display their talent.

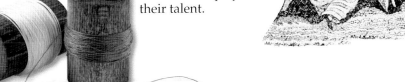

Italian hand

Gothic hand

Fashion

SACK DRESS
This popular colonial dress style was named for its back panel, shown here. The pleated fabric hung free from the shoulders, just like a sack.

Lace cuffs were removable for easy cleaning.

When ten-year-old Anna Green Winslow arrived in Boston to attend school, she wrote home to her mother in the country: *Dear Mama, You don't know the fashion here—I beg to look like other folk. What a stir would be made were I to make my appearance in my red Dominie & Black hat!* A Dominie (DOH-min-ee)—a plain dress worn on Sundays—was fine for the country, but in fashionable Boston a gentlewoman needed to dress in style. From silk slippers to poufy petticoats, dressing was an art—and also a chore!

Cane supports

FALSE HIPS
Women tied pocket hoops like saddlebags around their hips to make their skirts look fashionably full.

Eyelets for lacing corset

A new stomacher gave a gown a whole new look.

STOMACHERS
Stiff stomachers kept the *bodice*, or chest, of a dress smooth. Stomachers also helped with posture—they made it hard to slouch!

Delicate lace and bright silk for rosettes were imported from England.

Fringed edge spreads over hips.

This shoe was hand embroidered.

SILK SLIPPERS
A gentlewoman's shoes might be beautiful, but they weren't very comfortable. They lacked arch supports, which made walking any distance difficult.

NO TANNING ALLOWED!
Tans and freckles were not at all fashionable for proper colonial women and girls. They kept their heads covered at all times.

INDISPENSABLE
Colonial gowns did not have sewn-in pockets, so women and girls carried small handbags like this one, called an *indispensable*.

A drawstring cord wrapped around the wrist.

BUTTON UP!
Buttons could sometimes be miniature works of art—on both women's and men's clothes.

FAINT HELP
Fanning cool, fresh air around the head helped women overcome the dizziness they felt from wearing corsets.

Artists sometimes painted elaborate scenes on fans.

SQUEEZE!
Tightly laced corsets gave women stylishly small waists. But if a corset was pulled too tight, it could cause dizziness. Some women fainted because they simply couldn't get enough air.

A HEAD FOR HEIGHTS
As this cartoon shows, one extreme fashion was a towering headdress. Wool padding set on a wire frame was greased, powdered, and covered with lace and ribbons.

Anna Green Winslow wrote about her headdress in her diary: "It makes my head itch & ache & burn like anything!"

From the book *Felicity's Surprise*

Learning to Dance

Learning to dance was an important social skill for many gentlemen and ladies—at least in the southern colonies. Dance masters traveled from plantation to plantation to give dance lessons, much like the one Felicity attended at the Governor's Palace.

A tutor named Philip Fithian wrote about a dance master, Mr. Christian, who visited plantations in Virginia. The master's arrival meant all regular studies were dropped. Everyone had to attend the dance lesson. Philip watched, but he politely refused to dance. He was too embarrassed to admit that he had never learned how!

Mr. Christian is so strict indeed that he struck two of the young Misses for a fault in the course of their performance, even in the presence of the Mother of one of them! Philip Fithian 1773

4:30 P.M.
A dancing evening began with a meal. The ladies dined first. Then the servants reset the table, the gentlemen took their seats, and the meal began again.

6:00 P.M.
While the men ate, the ladies chatted on the terrace. Some strolled through the gardens, waiting for the dancing to begin.

7:00 P.M.
All dances began with *honors*, a polite bow and curtsy.

Felicity danced to piano sonatas by Wolfgang Amadeus Mozart and string quartets by Franz Joseph Haydn.

9:00 P.M.
Throughout the evening, the music
became more lively. Partners formed lines
to dance reels or joined hands to whirl
to the music of a spirited jig.

7:00 P.M. TO 8:00 P.M.
The first and most important dance at the
ball was the *minuet* (min-yu-WET). While the
other guests watched, one couple at a time danced
a minuet. They displayed their social grace in
their skillful performance.

PROPER PLAYING
Today, girls might play the
violin or French horn, but
Felicity wasn't allowed
to. Colonial gentlefolk
thought it ungraceful
for a young lady to
bend her neck or
pucker her lips.

2:00 A.M.
Drivers arrived to take
the ball guests home. The next
afternoon, many guests returned
for a second day of dancing!

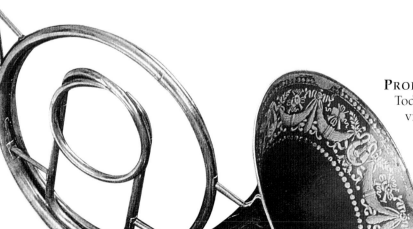

Courtship

A ball was a chance for young ladies and gentlemen to meet. They also met in everyday places—churches, schools, and shops. If a boy took a fancy to a girl, he began to *court* her, or spend time with her to show his affection. Courting couples talked and laughed while sledding, boating along a river, or riding through the woods. Often, courting led to a promise of marriage.

FLOWERS OF LOVE
Gifts of flower bouquets have long been a part of courting and marriage traditions. Pansies are symbols of "tender thoughts."

LOVE TOKEN
Colonial valentines were made by hand, and they were so treasured that families saved them for generations. This lacy paper valentine has survived for over two hundred years!

WEDDING RECORD
Families created beautiful private records of weddings. They often pictured a family tree, which the couple would fill in as time passed.

WEDDING COOKIES

Couples didn't have one wedding cake—they had hundreds! Cookies, called *cakes* back then, were stacked high and served to guests.

SPECIAL COLORS

Yellow was the most popular color for a wedding dress in the early 1700s. It was often mixed with blue, which symbolized *constancy*, or loyalty.

WEDDING BANDS

Women of Felicity's time rarely wore wedding bands. Those who did were likely to wear them on any finger, including the thumb!

BRIDE'S RANSOM

The young men at a country wedding watched for a chance to steal the bride's shoe. The groom then had to pay the thief a dollar to get back the slipper!

AN ELEGANT CEREMONY

By the late 1700s, white, which symbolized purity and goodness, was becoming popular for weddings. This formal wedding portrait shows the bride in white and a bridesmaid in blue.

STOCKING TOSS

In another country-wedding tradition, the ladies turned their backs to the bride and tossed rolled-up stockings. If one of the stockings struck the bride, the lady who threw it would supposedly be the next to marry.

*Stockings were held up by **garters**, or ribbons tied around the leg.*

George and Martha's Wedding

Colonel George Washington was a tall and handsome tobacco planter. But he had been unlucky in love. At least one woman had turned down his marriage proposal. His luck, however, was about to change.

One day while traveling to Williamsburg on important business, the colonel met an old friend, Major Chamberlayne, at a ferry crossing. The major invited George to dine with him. When George politely refused, Major Chamberlayne exclaimed, "Oh, but the loveliest widow in all Virginia is at this moment under my roof."

George handed his horse's reins to Bishop, his servant. "Have the horses ready to leave this afternoon," he said.

The widow was Martha Dandridge Custis. She was wealthy and very well mannered. On the day George Washington came to dine, Martha welcomed his company. Her two young children needed a father. The colonel had an excellent reputation. Their conversation continued well after dinner.

As the sun set, Bishop waited with the horses as instructed, but the colonel did not appear. *'Tis very strange*, Bishop thought. Never before had the colonel missed an appointment. Bishop did not know that a courtship had begun. In fact, George Washington would soon propose marriage to Martha—and she would accept.

The wedding of the colonel and the widow on January 6, 1759, was a grand social affair. Planters from the surrounding countryside came with their wives and daughters, all dressed in gowns and lace. The bride wore an embroidered white satin petticoat and a silk skirt with threads of silver. Her hair and neck were dressed with pearls. Diamonds decorated the buckles on her high-heeled satin slippers.

Washington was married in a coat of blue cloth with a vest of white satin. A gallant dress sword hung from his side. Old Cully, one of Martha's slaves, said of the groom on his wedding day, "None look'd like the man himself. So tall, so straight! . . . He set a horse and rode with such an air!"

After the wedding, a week of parties passed before George and Martha could politely leave their friends. Then Martha, in a velvet and fur traveling suit, stepped into a coach drawn by six horses. George rode alongside, tall and proud. For their honeymoon, they went to Williamsburg to attend meetings of Virginia's government! Martha was an honored guest. She and George had never been happier.

From Day to Day

Girls were their mothers' helpers in *housewifery*, the art of managing a household. In the colony of Connecticut, a girl named Abigail Foote helped her mother by doing everything from breaking up homemade cheese curds in a cheese basket to *hackeling*, or separating, fibers of the flax plant into threads. Just part of a single day's entry in Abigail's diary shows: *Fix'd gown—Mend Mother's Riding-hood—Spun short thread—Pleated and ironed—Spooled a piece—Milked the cows—Spun linen—Set a Red dye—Carded two pounds of whole wool—Spun harness twine—Scoured the pewter . . .* Each day had its own tasks, and the changing seasons brought new responsibilities, too.

Apples had to be peeled, cored, and sliced before they could be made into rich, sweet apple butter.

Hard for children—and animals—to resist!

Women made fruit last through the winter by drying it or boiling it to make jam.

SPRING
Spring was the time to pluck geese. A picker slipped a stocking or a basket over a goose's head so it couldn't bite, then plucked feathers right from the live bird! The feathers grew back to be harvested again.

Families raised geese for their feathers, not their meat. The feathers made a warm stuffing for pillows and mattresses.

SUMMER
Summer harvest brought fresh melons, peaches, apples, parsnips, carrots, and rhubarb to the table. Colonists also collected wild plants, like mushrooms and raspberries.

Cabbage and corn popular fresh vegeta Corn was also dried stored for use in the wi

There was plenty to harvest in fall. Corn, dried in shocks, was ready to be stored for animal feed in winter. And pumpkins, introduced to the settlers by Indians, were finally ripe.

After an animal was butchered, large cuts of meat were rolled in coarse sea salt. The salt helped to dry out the meat and keep it from rotting.

A girl might practice stitches on her sampler in the evening, after her mending work was done.

Carding wool took hours of patient work, scraping the combs back and forth to work the tangles out of the wool.

AUTUMN

Autumn was the killing time. Men and women killed and butchered farm animals. Then they smoked and salted the meat to preserve it for eating throughout the winter.

Autumn was candle-dipping time, too. Lengths of string were dipped into **tallow**, or melted beef fat, left to harden, then dipped again and again until the candle was thick enough to use.

WINTER

In winter, work was done indoors. It was time to spin wool into cloth and to sew new clothes and bed linens. Wool was *carded*, or pulled between combs, into fleecy balls, then drawn into thread on the spinning wheel.

Carded wool, ready for the spinning wheel

Managing a Household

It was a gentlewoman's responsibility to manage her family's home. Well-to-do women had lots of help. A gentlewoman named Elizabeth Drinker managed a large home in the busy city of Philadelphia. Her husband was a successful merchant. Mrs. Drinker hired servants to do the washing, baking, sewing, painting—just about everything!

TENDING THE LINENS
A free black woman hired by Mrs. Drinker washed and ironed clothes and linens each week. Linens were stored on shelves in a clothes press. Colonial homes had very few closets.

WASHERWOMAN
Mrs. Drinker hired an extra washerwoman when she cleaned the house from top to bottom. Laundry was carried out to the washhouse, a *dependency*, or separate building on the Drinkers' property.

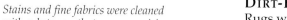

Stains and fine fabrics were cleaned with substances that seem surprising today—buttermilk, turpentine, lemon juice, gin, or eggs!

(1) *Mirrors were angled to reflect the brightest light from a fireplace and candles.*

(2) *A servant rubbed beeswax into wood furniture to create a protective coat.*

DIRT-FREE
Rugs were unusual in colonial homes.
There were no vacuums, so they were hard to keep clean.
The entry might have a painted floor mat, which was easily mopped.

UNDER CONTRACT

Indentured servants signed contracts to work for free for a set amount of time. Sometimes they worked to pay off a debt. Some had sold themselves to shipmasters in Europe in exchange for a trip to America. The shipmaster then sold them to a colonist, like Mr. Drinker.

Beds were draped with warm, heavy hangings in winter and mosquito netting in summer.

There was no running water in colonial times. Servants filled washbasins daily.

BEDBUGS

At least once a year, a servant "debugged" the bedsteads. Small insects called *bedbugs* could infest a house and carry dangerous diseases.

③ *Fireplace soot settled in every corner. Sweeping out ashes and dusting was a daily chore.*

KITCHEN

Many colonial homes had a separate dependency for the kitchen. But in crowded cities like Philadelphia, there just wasn't enough room.

④ *Servants painted the outside walls with a mixture of powdered white limestone and water, called whitewash.*

Mrs. Drinker treated her servants as part of her family. She knit warm socks for them and cut cloth for their underwear. "A dull day," she wrote in her diary. "I spent it in the kitchen cutting out underments for our blacks and whites. . . ."

Plantation Village

L ife and work on a southern plantation like Felicity's grandfather's was very different from life in a big northern city like Philadelphia. A plantation had many outbuildings and thousands of acres of land. Instead of servants to help run the place, hundreds of African slaves and white hired workers lived on the plantation. Mount Vernon, George Washington's plantation along the Potomac River in Virginia, had 8,000 acres and five separate working farms!

① BLACKSMITH'S SHOP
The blacksmith heated iron and shaped it into tools. His shop was far from the main house because smoke poured from the shop and hammers rang out endlessly.

②③ COACH HOUSE AND BARN
The stable hand kept carriages, carts, harnesses, saddles, and more in the coach house. The stable hand lived inside, ready at a moment's notice to saddle up a horse from the barn.

④ DOVECOTE
Doves were raised in a special house called a *dovecote.* They were considered even better to eat than chickens.

⑤ CHICKEN COOP
One colonial cake recipe called for 30 eggs! That sounds like a lot, but 30 eggs in Felicity's day wasn't the same as 30 eggs today. Chickens were much smaller in 1774, and their eggs were smaller, too.

⑥ OFFICE
The plantation owner carried on all his business here, meeting with the overseer, slave traders, merchants, and more. Some of these men were not welcome in the house because of their rough manners.

⑦ KITCHEN
The kitchen was separate from the main house because it was hot and smoky!

⑧ WELL
The well was placed close to the washhouse, kitchen, and house so no one would need to lug buckets of water too far.

16 WHARF

Most plantations were built along rivers and had access to a wharf large enough to dock ships. Plantation owners could receive goods from England and ship crops overseas.

15 KITCHEN GARDEN

A plantation supplied all of its own produce. In the kitchen garden, peas, asparagus, lettuce, beets, broccoli, strawberries, and more grew in plenty.

14 SLAVE QUARTERS

Small cabins housed the slaves who maintained the gardens, workshops, and main house. The field slaves were housed in cabins even farther from the main house.

13 THE NECESSARY

The *necessary*, or outdoor toilet, was located a good distance from the house— for both privacy and cleanliness.

12 SPINNING HOUSE

Cotton, flax, and hemp were grown in the plantation fields. Twelve or more women were constantly at work spinning, weaving, and knitting to supply all the cloth for the plantation.

11 SMOKEHOUSE

Colonists kept meat from spoiling by smoking it. The smokehouse had a dirt floor where a fire burned, and no windows or chimney so smoke stayed inside.

9 DAIRY

The dairy had vents just beneath the roof to help keep air moving, which cooled the milk, butter, and cream stored inside.

10 WASHHOUSE

Steamy tubs full of sudsy water bubbled over a fire in the washhouse. The laundress scrubbed, rinsed, and wrung the clothes by hand and hung them on racks to dry. Then she mended, starched, ironed, and folded them!

Drying racks

Working Hands

The large plantations in the southern colonies produced rice, cotton, and tobacco. Some white indentured servants tended the crops for the landowner. But by the 1770s, black field hands did most of the work. Black people hoed rows of cotton. Black people planted tobacco seedlings in the fields in spring, weeded the plants in summer, and harvested the leaves in autumn. These people—men, women, and even children—were not free. They were slaves. In colonial times, it was not against the law to keep slaves or even to hurt them.

WHIPS AND WORK
A white overseer controlled a master's slaves, watching their work in the fields. He carried a whip. He would snap it across the back of a man, woman, or child if he thought the slave needed a reason to work harder or faster.

SHACKLED AND SHIPPED
Africans were shackled together and forced onto ships bound for plantation country to be sold as slaves. They were held below deck, where the smell alone made them sick. Each slave was worth money to the slave trader. But often more than half of a slave ship's "cargo" died while at sea.

SLAVE QUARTERS
Near Williamsburg, Robert Carter owned 60,000 acres of land and 600 slaves. He thought of himself as a kind master. He fed and clothed his slaves and provided shacks like these for their homes.

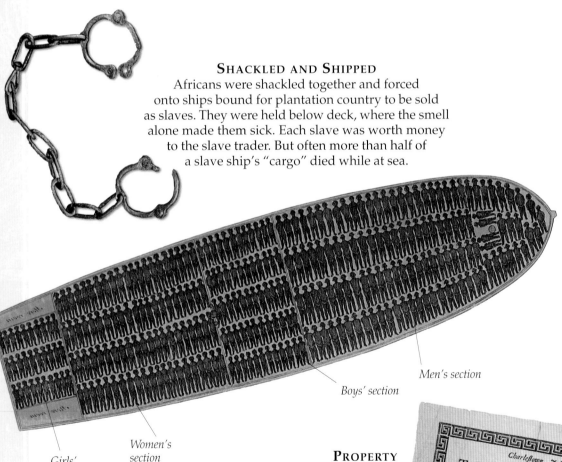

Men's section

Boys' section

Women's section

Girls' section

PROPERTY
Once a slave ship docked in America, the trader sold the men, women, and children. By law, they became the property of the master who bought them.

Charlestown, July 24th, 1769.
TO BE SOLD,
On THURSDAY the third Day
of August next,
A CARGO
OF
NINETY-FOUR
PRIME, HEALTHY
NEGROES,
CONSISTING OF
Thirty-nine Men

THE RACK
If a slave tried to run away and was caught, she might have to wear a rack of bells on her head. Then she could not make a single move without alerting everyone around.

From the book *Happy Birthday, Felicity!*

FREEMEN
Free blacks like Isaac worked for pay. By a slave's standards, they were lucky. But they did not have the same rights that white colonists had. Just like a slave, Isaac had to stay off the streets at night. No one would check to see if he was a free black rather than a slave before arresting him.

SOLD!

TO BE SOLD,
A likely ſtrong Negro Girl, about 17 Years of Age ; ſold by Reaſon that a Boy would ſuit the Owner better. Enquire at R. & S. *Draper's* Printing Office

Slave owners often sold their slaves, separating husbands and wives and children from one another. Young Mary Prince knew the pain of being separated from her family. Her master wanted to marry. To raise money for the wedding, he decided to sell three of his slaves—Mary and two of her sisters. Master Williams also owned Mary's mother, but she would stay behind. Mary never forgot the day Master Williams took her to the public auction, or *vendue* (vahn-DO). Years later she wrote:

Master Williams took me by the hand, and led me out into the middle of the street and turned me slowly round. I was soon examined and handled in the same manner that a butcher would a calf or a lamb he was about to purchase. The masters talked about me as if I could no more understand their meaning than a dumb beast. I then saw my sisters led forth, and sold to different owners. When the sale was over, my mother hugged and kissed us, and mourned over us, begging us to keep up a good heart.

Breaking the Code

Each colony had its own *slave codes*, or laws that controlled the lives of slaves. In North Carolina, slaves could not hold property. Nor could they buy, sell, or even give away anything without the permission of their master or overseer. Georgia's slave codes said that a master would be fined if he or she allowed a slave to work for another person and receive payment. The laws made it almost impossible for a slave to earn money to buy his or her freedom. But not all slave owners agreed with the laws. And not all slaves obeyed the laws.

CHOICES
In most states it was illegal for slaves to get an education. Yet in Boston, tailor John Wheatley freed his house slave Phillis, taught her to read English and Latin, and schooled her in classical literature. Phillis published her first poem at age 14.

JUMPING THE BROOM
These slaves may be about to "jump the broom." Many colonies did not allow slaves to marry. But slaves performed their own marriage ceremonies. A bride and groom jumped over a broomstick together to become husband and wife in the eyes of other slaves and each oth

SCHOOLING
Philadelphian Anthony Benezet taught white people during the day and black people at night. He tried to convince people that blacks and whites were equal in intelligence, and argued for an end to slavery.

GARDENS OF PLENTY
Slaves often weren't allowed to sell anything, not even the vegetables they grew in their tiny garden plots. But sometimes they secretly traded with other slaves for meat or flour or tools.

NIGHT-WALKING
Enslaved husbands, wives, and children were often sold away from one another. Although forbidden to travel after dark, many slaves walked over miles of foot trails at night to visit one another. Some wrote fake "passes" to use in case they were caught.

A jawbone rattle was held by the tip and tapped with a stick, shaken like a tambourine to rattle the teeth, or scraped to produce a rumbling sound.

DRUMMING
In the evenings, drumbeats from slaves' quarters echoed over the fields to neighboring plantations. The drumbeats were codes slaves developed to send messages. They could even tell of plans for escape.

"Am I Not a Man and a Brother?"

By 1776, America was at war with England. The royal governor of Virginia gave enslaved Africans a choice: any slave who joined the Loyalist army would be given his freedom. Within weeks, three hundred slaves ran away from their masters to join.

Many people began to question slavery during the war. The Declaration of Independence said that all men were created equal. How could that not include slaves? This image of a shackled slave asking to be recognized as a human being, with the same feelings and abilities as anyone else, became an *abolitionist*, or antislavery, symbol. Slaves and abolitionists would fight for freedom for nearly a hundred more years.

MUSIC AND RHYTHM
Music was not only a form of entertainment and worship, it also kept slaves' spirits up and their hopes for freedom alive. Slaves carved the dry bones of animals into instruments that clicked and tapped and whistled, and turned wood and leather into booming drums.

EGG MONEY
Some owners did give permission for their slaves to sell their own goods, such as vegetables and eggs. It would take years, but a slave might earn enough money to buy his or her freedom.

Colonial coins

Slaves made drums like this one out of American cedar and deerskin.

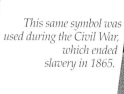

This same symbol was used during the Civil War, which ended slavery in 1865.

deliver me from the oppression of man.

Colonial Law

Even free men and women were not always permitted to say what they thought. The right to free speech didn't exist! People who spoke against the king could be charged with *slander*, or making false accusations. The idea that a person was innocent until proven guilty did not yet exist either. A person accused of a crime had to prove his or her innocence. The place to do that was inside a courthouse.

CRIME AND PUNISHMENT

Inside the courthouse, the king's court tried and sentenced debtors, like Jiggy Nye, and runaway apprentices, like Ben. Almost anyone could go to court and argue his or her case, although married women had to let their husbands argue for them.

PILLORIES

For crimes such as slander or drunkenness, men and women had their head and hands locked in a *pillory*. Pillories often stood in the courthouse yard, where mobs would gather to jeer at the criminals and pelt them with garbage.

PUBLIC LASHINGS

The guilty could also be tied to the pillory post, with their backs stripped bare. As a crowd watched, a public official would deliver a *lashing*, or whipping, striking at least 30 blows.

ELIZABETH CANNING,
Drawn from Life, as she stood at the Bar to receive her Sentence, in the Session's-House, in the *Old-Bailey*.

Women and the Law

THE FEME SOLE
Women without husbands were legally known as *feme soles*, French for single women. A feme sole could own property and run her own business. Her rights were similar to a man's. However, most women did not want to be *spinsters*, or women who never married. Spinsters were thought to be ugly and mean-spirited.

A cartoon of a spinster

STAFFORD,' *July* 6, 1772.

AS my Wife *Jean Johnson* is not contented to live with me, but goes on in such a Manner as I think is likely to ruin me and my Children, I do hereby forewarn all Persons from dealing or making any Bargain or Contract with her on my Account, for they may depend I will pay no Debt she contracts.

JOHN JOHNSON, Senior.

ORDERED TO THE COLONIES
Often people were sent to the colonies after being found guilty of crimes in England. That is what happened to Elizabeth Canning in 1754. The English courts found her guilty of *perjury*, or lying, and sentenced her to one month in jail and seven years as an indentured servant in the "uncivilized" colonies.

RUNAWAY WIVES
Women could not easily leave their husbands. Just why Jean Johnson fled from her husband is not clear. But John posted the newspaper advertisement above warning people that he would not pay any bills or debts she made.

GIBBETING
The worst crimes, such as murder, could be punished by hanging. Sometimes those who were hanged were also *gibbeted* (JIB-it-ed). Their bodies were put in a metal frame and displayed to the public.

BRANDINGS
A person found guilty of theft had a T burned into the flesh at the base of the right thumb. It showed every time the person shook hands.

A HUSBAND'S PROPERTY
Once a woman married, everything she owned became her husband's property. When Anne Campbell ran away from her husband, he said that his wife had "robbed" him of "all her wearing apparel." Poor Anne didn't even own her clothes!

31

Women In Charge

Many colonial women carried on business outside of their homes. They were an important part of public life. Women advertised their services in newspapers and with painted signs hung over their shop doors. A woman often ran her husband's business after his death or while he was away. In some northern colonies, there was even a legal term for such a woman. She was called a *deputy husband*.

A milliner sewed miniature versions of Europe's latest fashions for customers to choose from.

A tavern sign

SILVERSMITH
Silversmiths made silver spoons, bowls, candlesticks, and more. In a silversmith's shop, a grate on the floor caught silver dust so it could be melted down and used again.

TAVERN KEEPER
Many women ran taverns, offering beds, food, and entertainment for both gentlemen and ladies.

PRINTER
Mary Katherine Goddard was a printer who used paper made from cloth. She soaked the cloth, beat it to a pulp, then pressed it into thin sheets. The original Declaration of Independence was printed in Mary's shop.

MILLINER
Milliners sold everything from paper patterns and cloth to shoes, jewelry, clocks, and tableware. A milliner had to be skilled in sewing, tailoring, laundering, ironing, lace making, accounting, and bookkeeping.

A midwife handing a newborn to its father

MIDWIFE
Midwives helped deliver babies, and they were much respected for their skills. They were welcomed into every home, from the wealthiest to the poorest. Martha Ballard was a midwife in the northern wilderness of the New England colonies. In her lifetime she delivered more than 1,000 babies! She also treated all sorts of illnesses, from sore throats to smallpox.

True Blue

Eliza Lucas was just 16 when her father left his plantation to serve in the king's army. Colonel Lucas depended on his daughter to manage his plantation in his absence. Other girls Eliza's age were attending teas and dance parties, but she spent her days writing business letters and experimenting with plants. Since her mother had passed away, Eliza had had many responsibilities. She didn't mind at all. She loved her work. She was good at it, too. One of her plant experiments was a great success. The indigo seeds that her father sent home to her thrived! The seeds from the plant made fine blue dye cakes. Within a few years, Eliza's indigo dye brought new wealth to her father's plantation and to South Carolina, too. Although Eliza didn't know it yet, the crop would play an important role in the war for independence. The Patriots' Continental Army wore uniforms dyed with Eliza's indigo blue.

Daily Toilet

Thomas Jefferson gave his ten-year-old daughter Patsy instructions for her *daily toilet*, or grooming: *Be you, from the moment you rise till you go to bed, as cleanly and properly dressed as at the hours of dinner or tea. . . . Dress yourself in such a style, as that you may be seen by any gentleman without his being able to discover a pin amiss, or any other circumstance of neatness wanting.* But it wasn't easy to be so clean. Many colonists even believed that taking a bath was bad for your health!

HORN COMB
Women fastened their long hair in place with combs often made from cow horn.

HAND MIRROR
Mirrors were used to reflect light into a room more often than to let a girl see what she looked like. A small vanity mirror like this one was a luxury.

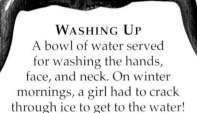

WASHING UP
A bowl of water served for washing the hands, face, and neck. On winter mornings, a girl had to crack through ice to get to the water!

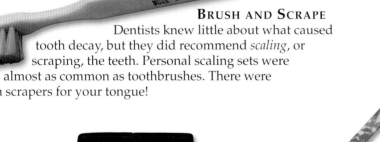

BRUSH AND SCRAPE
Dentists knew little about what caused tooth decay, but they did recommend *scaling*, or scraping, the teeth. Personal scaling sets were almost as common as toothbrushes. There were even scrapers for your tongue!

Tongue scraper

LICE COMB

Lice, tiny creatures that dig into the scalp and suck blood, were a common problem. Fine-tooth combs were used to remove the pests.

Pump handle

WIG POWDERER

Both men and women wore light-colored wigs in public. They were made of bleached animal hair, which faded and discolored easily. This powderer pumped puffs of flour to cover any dark spots.

Powder puffed from here.

CHAMBER POT

Chamber pots were indoor toilets. They were most often stored under a bed.

SCENTED CLOTH

Some handkerchiefs were sprinkled with lavender- or violet-scented water. If bothered by a foul smell, a lady could hide her disgust by gently pressing the cloth to her nose.

EYE BATH

An eye bath was part of every toiletry set. The bowl was filled with liquid and placed against the open eye. A lady held the bowl in place by the stem, and tilted her head back to wash her eye.

PERFUME BOTTLE

Because colonists hardly ever took baths, they used perfumes to cover up odors!

SHARING THE TUB

A colonial man named Henry Drinker liked to wash in the river when warm weather allowed. Mrs. Drinker, however, wrote in her diary that she had *not been wet all over at once, for 28 years past.* Mrs. Drinker was not unclean—most colonists did not wash their entire bodies all at once.

Then one day Henry Drinker brought something surprising home—a bathtub! Buckets of water were heated and then poured into it. Mrs. Drinker wrote in her diary: *I went into a warm bath this afternoon, Henry after me, Lydia and Patience, our servants, went into the same bath after him, and John after them.*

On some days, even Tartar, the family dog, shared the tub!

Healthy Humors

EVERY MAN HIS OWN DOCTOR
Most treatments for sickness began at home. This booklet gives "plain and easy recipes" to restore good health. Some recipes might have worked. Others couldn't have! For a cough, the cure is "riding on Horseback every Day."

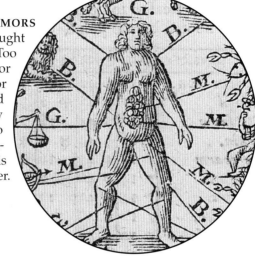

I n a world where keeping clean wasn't easy, diseases spread quickly. Doctors and midwives in Felicity's time believed the body contained four *humors*, or fluids. They thought the body had to have just the right amount of each fluid to be healthy. Too much of any one humor was believed to cause sickness. Getting rid of the extra fluid was supposed to cure the sickness. Today's doctors know that germs and bacteria—not too much fluid—cause sickness.

THE FOUR HUMORS
Too much blood brought on the red flush of fever. Too much *phlegm* (FLEM), or mucus, made people weak or sluggish. Angry people had too much *choler*, or yellow bile, and sad people had too much *melancholy* (MEL-en-kah-lee), or black bile. *Bile* is fluid made by the liver.

Air holes helped keep leeches alive.

LEECH JAR
If a doctor thought a patient had too much blood, he applied *leeches*, or blood-sucking worms, to the patient's skin. A child might be treated with two leeches, and an adult with twenty or more.

Pestle

Mortar

MORTAR AND PESTLE
Doctors ground herbs into *pukes*, or pastes, with a mortar and pestle. Patients swallowed the paste and soon began vomiting, which supposedly rid their bodies of too much bile.

PORTABLE MEDICINE CHEST
This chest held twelve medicine bottles and as much mixing and bandaging equipment as the doctor could squeeze into the lower drawer.

FATAL MISTAKE
Colonial surgeons believed the human body contained twelve quarts of blood. In fact, the body holds only six quarts. Doctors who bled patients too much brought them dangerously close to death.

GEORGE WASHINGTON
After George Washington left office as the first president of the United States, doctors treated his infected throat by bleeding him of four and a half quarts of blood in 24 hours. He died partly from the treatment meant to cure him.

BLOODLETTING KIT
Bloodletting was another way to get rid of extra blood. A doctor used a special knife called a *lancet* to slice open a vein. He drained the blood into a bleeding bowl, then closed the wound.

Lancets were made in different sizes and shapes in order to take more or less blood.

BARBER OR DOCTOR?
Barbers, or haircutters, also performed bloodletting. A barber's pole was originally meant to represent an arm, with the red stripes being blood and the round crown being the bleeding bowl.

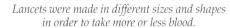

These bottles are clearly labeled, but many medicine bottles held nostrums, or mixes of secret ingredients "guaranteed" to cure various problems.

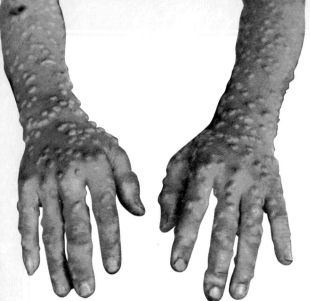

Outbreak of Sorrow

Pennsylvania Hospital

Outbreaks of a disease, or *epidemics* (ep-uh-DEM-iks), were dreaded in the colonies. Smallpox caused the most deaths. Smallpox was a *virus*, a tiny kind of germ that causes disease. Colonial doctors knew nothing of viruses or how to treat them. What they did know was that one sick person could quickly spread smallpox. Hundreds could become ill and die within weeks. Today, doctors know how to cure this deadly disease.

THE FIRST SIGNS

The first sign of smallpox was a high fever. Three or four days later, a red rash covered the face, the hands, and the soles of the feet. The red marks developed into bumps called *pox*.

Yesterday, about six o'clock P.M., my little grandson ascended to a better world. He had the smallpox by inoculation, but very full... Pity me, o my Friends, under this weight of sorrows! — *Mather Bayles, 1787*

AN
Historical ACCOUNT
OF THE
SMALL-POX
INOCULATED
IN
NEW ENGLAND,
Upon all Sorts of Perfons, *Whites, Blacks,*
and of all Ages and Conftitutions.

With fome Account of the Nature of the
Infection in the NATURAL and INOCULATED
Way, and their different Effects on HUMAN
BODIES.

With fome fhort DIRECTIONS to the Un-
EXPERIENCED in this Method of Practice.

...mbly dedicated to her Royal Highnefs the Princefs of WALES.
By *Zabdiel Boylston*, F. R. S.

The Second Edition, Corrected.

LONDON:
...d for S. CHANDLER, at the Crofs-Keys in the *Poultry.*
M. DCC. XXVI.
...ted at BOSTON in N. E. for S. GERRISH in
...il, and T. HANCOCK at the Bible and Three Crowns
...nftreet. M. DCC. XXX.

TAKING THE POX

Mather Bayles wrote of the death of his grandson after he "took the pox," or was *inoculated* (in-OK-yuh-lay-ted) with smallpox. Doctors passed a needle and thread through an infected pock, and then under the skin of a healthy person. The healthy person got a mild case of smallpox. If the person survived, he or she would never get smallpox again.

GRIEF

Children especially were at risk during epidemics. The mother in this painting lost her young daughter to smallpox.

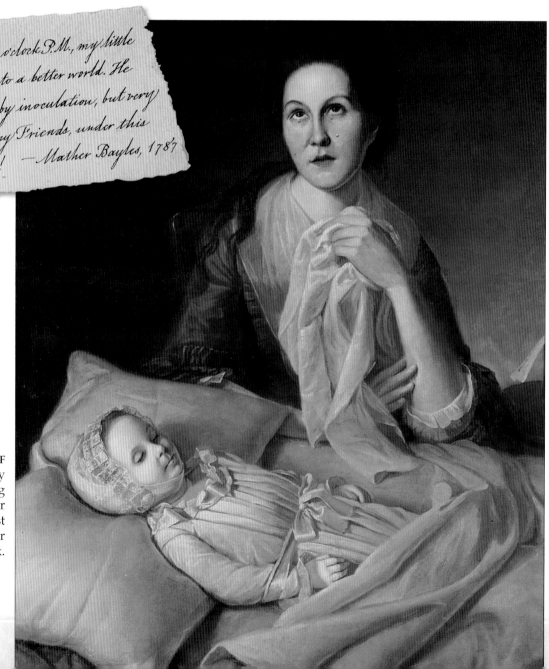

ISOLATION

Those who "took the pox" had to be *isolated* (ICE-oh-lay-ted), or kept apart, so they wouldn't spread the disease to anyone else. Many were shut up for weeks in a house or hospital. Some patients became very sick. Some even died. Parents had no way of knowing if their children would live after being inoculated.

BLACK WAX

Wax to seal letters came in many colors, but black meant only one thing— news of a death.

FUNERAL JEWELRY

Special rings, brooches, and necklace charms were made for funerals. They often bore the name of the dead and the date of death. Judge Samuel Sewall of Boston owned more than fifty such rings, each a memory of a lost friend or relative.

MOURNING CLOTHES

If people could afford to buy the fabric, they wore black *mourning*, or grieving, clothes. Black fabric also draped the windows of the dead person's home and lined the casket.

DEATH CARTS

During an epidemic, so many people died each day in the cities that caretakers piled the bodies on carts and took them away for burial. The dead could still infect the living, so there were no funeral arrangements.

DEATH VISITS

The tombstone of Susanna Jayne, who died of smallpox, shows Death crowned with a wreath of leaves. The image suggests that Death has won over life. During epidemics, Death seemed to be everywhere.

Never to Return . . .

For weeks, Thomas Jefferson's wife, Martha, lay in bed, too weak to move. She'd recently given birth to a healthy baby girl, and she wasn't recovering. Day after day, Thomas and their ten-year-old daughter Patsy nursed Martha. They were never beyond her calling. When Thomas was not sitting beside Martha's bed, he was in a small room next door, writing at a desk.

One afternoon, Martha wrote a few words from a story she had read called *Tristam Shandy: The days and hours pass over our heads like clouds of a windy day never to return . . .*

She was too weak to continue. When Thomas found the paper and read what she had written, he picked up his pen and finished the paragraph, which he recognized. It talked about the *"eternal separation which we are shortly to make."*

Thomas knew his wife was soon to die. He folded her paper and slipped it into a private drawer in his desk.

Days later, Martha Jefferson passed away. She probably died from a disease that no one in colonial times understood how to treat—diabetes.

Thomas's grief was so great he fainted. Later, he shut himself up in his room. Still, Patsy could hear what she called "the violence of his emotions." Now it was the young daughter who had to nurse the father. She went to his room and did not leave him. He paced constantly, lying down only when he got too tired to keep walking. When at last he stepped outside, he mounted his horse and rode endlessly, over roads and through woods. Patsy rode with him. Only she could reach through her father's terrible grief and bring him home.

Thomas Jefferson did not marry again. Some people believed that he had promised his wife as she lay dying that he would not marry. That may be only a romantic story. But this much is true: Years later, a folded piece of paper was found in a desk drawer in Thomas Jefferson's home. Its worn edges proved that it had been opened and read and folded away again many, many times. It was the paragraph from *Tristam Shandy* that Martha and Thomas had written together. Between the folds was a lock of Martha's hair.

Rebellion!

Disease killed thousands of people in the American colonies in the 1770s. But even more lives were about to be lost—not to disease but to war. The trouble between the colonists and King George had grown worse. Patriots began to prepare for war by storing gunpowder and weapons in village storehouses, called *magazines*. In 1775, British soldiers, or *regulars*, began raiding the storehouses, stealing the supplies to weaken the Patriots.

DRUMS AND BELLS

Soon, the beating of drums and the ringing of bells sounded an alarm throughout all the colonies. Terrifying rumors spread like wildfire. Some Patriots thought the British planned to murder them in their sleep!

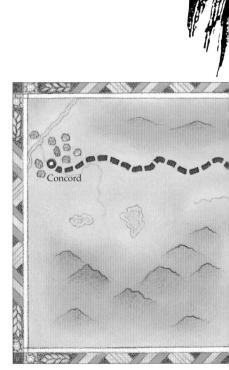

From the book *Happy Birthday, Felicity!*

SOUND THE ALARM!

War came to Williamsburg in the spring of 1775. Late one night, British marines tried to steal the colonists' gunpowder. No one knows for certain who sounded the alarm that night. It was not the only alarm sounded in the colonies in 1775.

A SIGNAL

In Massachusetts, Patriots learned the British planned to march from Boston to Concord to take supplies. A Patriot spy was sent to find out the troops' route. From the bell tower of Boston's tallest church, the spy was to light one lantern if the troops took the long land route, two if they went by sea.

MIDNIGHT RIDE

On the night of April 18, 1775, the Patriots watched for the lantern signal. When it came—two lanterns—they were ready. Paul Revere rode throughout the countryside, shouting, "Make haste! The regulars are coming!"

Concord

MINUTEMEN
Minutemen were Patriots who promised to defend the villages in "a minute's notice." The night of April 19, they hurried out with guns, bayonets, and even hatchets to meet the British.

OFF TO BATTLE
The minutemen tried to stop the British at Lexington, Massachusetts. Many women saw their husbands off to battle. Then they took their children and fled to a safer place a mile from town. Throughout the day, they heard distant guns. Not every husband would return.

UNSTOPPABLE?
The British were well trained and well equipped, marching in columns that seemed unstoppable. They marched right through Lexington, leaving eight Patriots dead. But in Concord, the minutemen held their ground. The British had to retreat, and twice as many British died as colonists.

Off to War

When news of the battles in Lexington and Concord reached King George, he ordered 300 supply ships and 30 battleships to New York. Revolution had begun. Soon the Patriots' Declaration of Independence would make it official. It was a declaration of war. But the Patriots had no navy and no army to fight against the British. They turned to George Washington, asking him to organize and lead a new Continental Army. Washington was worried. What if he should fail? But he accepted his new role. He chose to fight for liberty. Each colonist faced the same fear, and each decided whether to fight for liberty or remain loyal to the king.

The smell of war began to be pretty strong, but I was determined to have no hand in it, happen when it might. I felt myself to be a coward. What — venture my carcass where bullets fly? Stay at home out of harm's way, thought I.

Joseph Plumb Martin, 1774

OFF TO WAR
Joseph Plumb Martin was 14 when he wrote these words in his diary. Unlike Ben in Felicity's stories, he did not want to join the militia. But Joseph did finally enlist. As he prepared to leave for war, he wrote, *"I have my gun, my knapsack, my blanket . . . Will I be able to kill someone else?"*

KNAPSACK
Soldiers had to bring their own supplies. They packed knapsacks with all they could carry. They did not know that the war would drag on for seven long years.

KEEPSAKE
Soldiers knew they might never see their loved ones again. They packed *miniatures*, tiny portrait paintings, to remember them by.

JOIN, or DIE.

DIVIDED WE FALL
Posters like this one urged boys and men from all the colonies to join together in the fight for freedom. Each set of initials stands for a colony. "N.E." stands for the six New England colonies.

Firelock

Trigger

DRINKING WATER
A wooden canteen was essential. Soldiers never knew when they would next see fresh water, and long marches through the countryside left every soldier weak from thirst.

HARD MEALS
Biscuits called *hardtack*, hard cheese, and dried beef were easy to carry and lasted a long time. Most soldiers ate hardtack day after day. It was all they had.

MUSIC BOYS
The youngest boys to enlist, between 12 and 16 years old, were usually put to work as drummers or fifers, keeping the troops marching in time.

CAMP GEAR
A soldier was lucky to have his own mug, silverware, or cooking utensils. It wasn't only food that was scarce. All supplies were few and far between.

FAITH
Bibles were a much-needed source of strength and encouragement.

BROWN BESS
The Brown Bess was the most popular gun among soldiers. To load it, a soldier pulled back the firelock and measured powder into the pan inside the gun. Then he jammed a bullet cartridge into the barrel with the ramrod. When he pulled the trigger, the powder caught fire and exploded, forcing the cartridge out of the barrel.

POWDER HORN
Every soldier carried a powder horn. The tip of the horn was used to measure powder and pour it into the musket.

THE
HOLY BIBLE,
CONTAINING THE
Old and New Testaments:
TOGETHER WITH THE
APOCRYPHA:
TRANSLATED OUT OF THE
Original Tongues,
AND
WITH THE FORMER TRANSLATIONS DILIGENTLY
COMPARED AND REVISED,
BY THE
Special Command of King JAMES I, of ENGLAND.

SECOND WORCESTER EDITION.

Barrel

Ramrod

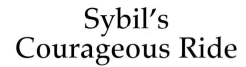

Women at War

Mary Hays

Mary Hays's husband

Women were not allowed to fight as soldiers in the war. Still, some women found a way. Many disguised themselves as men. Other women found themselves in battle almost by accident. When Mary Ludwig Hays saw her husband wounded, she promptly took his place. While she was bending down to reach for a cartridge, a cannon shot from the enemy passed directly between her legs! Private Joseph Martin saw Mary Hays in action. He wrote later in his diary: *No other damage was done than carrying away all the lower part of her petticoat*!

MOLLY PITCHER
Women who joined their husbands along the battlefront were sometimes called Molly Pitchers. They risked their lives to carry pitchers of water to the troops during battle.

EMILY GEIGER
Emily Geiger served in secret. This southern lady agreed to deliver an important letter to a Patriot general. But British scouts captured her on the road. They suspected she was a spy. They left her alone while they found a woman to search her clothing. Quickly, Emily memorized the letter. Then she ate it, piece by piece!

Sybil's Courageous Ride

More than anything, 16-year-old Sybil Ludington wanted to be a Patriot soldier. Each day as she exercised Star, her family's spirited stallion, she dreamed of riding in her father's regiment. But women were not allowed to fight as soldiers in the war.

Finally, on the night of April 26, 1777, Sybil got her chance. A tired rider brought a message to her father. British troops had set fire to the nearby city of Danbury, Connecticut! As Colonel Ludington looked toward Danbury, he saw that the sky was red from the fire. He knew it was up to his men to stop the British. But who would make the dangerous night ride through the countryside to summon the soldiers? The messenger was exhausted, and Colonel Ludington had to stay and make battle plans.

"I will go," Sybil said quickly. Trying to keep the eagerness out of her voice, she added, "I can handle Star better than anyone, and I know the whole territory."

When her father agreed, Sybil's heart leaped. She was nervous, but she knew she and Star could take care of each other. Sybil and her famil

At the first farmhouse Sybil came to, doors flew open at the sound of Star's hoofbeats. "Muster at Ludington's!" she shouted and rode on. She rode from farm to farm, pounding on doors and shouting her message. By the time she was halfway through, her cloak was caked with mud and her throat ached from crying out. But she and Star could not stop. Every soldier in her father's regiment must be told.

Once during their ride, Sybil heard hoofbeats and feared they might be British soldiers. She trembled as she and Star waited off the path while the riders passed only a few feet in front of them. Shaken, she led Star back to the path. *We have to keep going*, she thought. *There are more men to alert.*

By the time Sybil reached home, her voice was gone and she was exhausted. She and Star had ridden more than 40 miles in three hours. But when she rode into her yard, she saw more than 400 men, ready to march. *It was worth it*, she thought as she was carried to bed.

The men Sybil had mustered were able to stop the British. They drove the British back to their ships on Long Island Sound. Soon after Sybil's ride, General George Washington paid a visit to thank her for her courageous deed. Sybil's brave ride for independence had made her a hero in her own time.

went out to the barn. Her brothers saddled Star, and her mother put a cape around Sybil to protect her from the wind and rain. Sybil swung up on Star. She listened carefully to her father's directions and repeated them word for word. She saluted her father and turned onto the path. She was off!

The War at Home

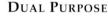

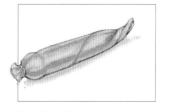

The thunder of cannon fire echoed off the battlefields and into the nearby villages and cities. Some families—Loyalist and Patriot alike—fled to safer places in the countryside. But not all. When husbands and sons went to war, many women stayed behind to manage plantations and farms and village shops. Some who stayed did not wish to choose sides. It was war they were against, not the British or the Americans. But no one could escape the violence of the Revolution.

LIBERTY KERCHIEF

This cotton handkerchief honors the hard work of women whose husbands were fighting. Around the border are 13 scenes of three sisters at work—spinning and weaving cloth for the soldiers, taking food to camps, and running the farm.

DOING THE DISHES

Women at home helped the war effort by melting down their pewter and lead dishes, cups, and candlesticks. Then they made the molten metal into musket balls.

DUAL PURPOSE

A Concord woman named Melicent Barret used her sewing scissors to make musket cartridges at home. Melicent's cartridges were rushed straight to the minutemen as the British approached.

ARMING THE ARMY

Women heated musket ball molds like this one over a fire and then pressed the two halves together. They poured molten lead or pewter into the small holes on either side of the mold. Once the mold cooled, they opened it and knocked out the musket balls.

Molten pewter or lead poured in here.

MAKING A MUSKET CARTRIDGE

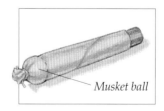

Musket ball

First, women placed paper or fabric under a *former*, or a hollow tube about six inches long. They rolled up the former in the paper one inch from the paper's edge.

Next, they placed a musket ball in the end of the paper roll beneath the former and tied the tube shut with twine or thread.

Finally, they poured in an explosive powder, removed the former, and twisted and tied the end to secure the powder charge.

*The first scene shows the women alone. They determine to do the **husbandry**, or men's work, themselves.*

The final scene shows a happy ending. The families are safely reunited after the war.

FIELDS AFLAME

When Patriot Catherine Schuyler heard that British regulars were headed for her farm, she acted quickly. Her farm's wheat fields were ready for harvesting. They would be a rich prize for the British. She took a torch and set fire to the grain.

GOLD AND LINEN

A Patriot woman named Esther Reed organized "The Association." This group of women asked for donations of gold dollars and used the money to buy linen. They sewed more than 2,000 shirts and delivered them to Washington's troops.

SHATTERED PEACE

Some colonists were *Quakers*, a religious group that believes war is wrong. They did not fight, but that did not save them from violence. Quaker Henry Drinker refused to close his shop on July 4 to celebrate the colonies' declaration of independence— and war. Angry neighbors threw bricks through his windows.

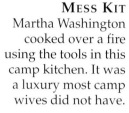

Camp F•llowers

Most women stayed home during the war, but thousands of others joined the troops of both the Continental and British armies. Many were the widows and wives of enlisted men whose homes and farms had been destroyed. They had nowhere else to go. The armies welcomed these camp followers. They carried equipment, cooked and cleaned for the men, bandaged their wounds, and mended their torn clothes.

SOLDIERS' AID
Officers' wives spent their time in camp knitting mittens, gloves, and stockings, mending uniforms, and carrying baskets of food or home remedies to the tents of sick soldiers.

LAUNDRY
Lower-ranking soldiers' wives and widows most often served as laundresses. The clothes of the wounded, sick, and dead were all washed time and again. Many men— and women—wore little more than rags.

ARMY HOSPITALS
Tents were turned into temporary hospitals. Women helped surgeons with every procedure.

MESS KIT
Martha Washington cooked over a fire using the tools in this camp kitchen. It was a luxury most camp wives did not have.

Serving platter

Tins stored any fresh foods.

Spice shakers

AMMUNITION WIVES
Camp followers carried all sorts of supplies. Some carried precious musket balls and pellets. They were called "ammunition wives."

IRON KETTLE
It was usually the women who carried the cookware. Many items were abandoned because they were too heavy. An army's route could often be traced by following the heavy iron kettles left by the roadside.

CASES OF CHAMPAGNE
The women and children of the British officers traveled together in wagons and gun carriages. Baroness von Riedesel refused to travel without her 30 cases of champagne and trunks of clothing for herself, her three children, and her servants.

Baroness von Riedesel

Martha Washington

A set of four kettles nested inside this pot.

MARTHA AT CAMP
Martha Washington had never been outside of Virginia before she joined her husband at his winter camp in Valley Forge, Pennsylvania. A young girl of 16 who went with Martha as she moved through the camp hospital wrote in her diary:

On one occasion she went to the hut of a dying sergeant, whose young wife was with him. Lady Washington knelt down by his straw pallet and prayed earnestly for him and his wife. I shall never forget the scene.

Bottles of wine and spirits were carried along. Wine was often safer than water to drink.

A Night to Remember

George Washington's worst fears had come true by December 1776. He had lost every major battle against the British. He had lost forts, gunpowder and cannon, and especially men. Most of the militia from the countryside refused to fight with Washington's Continental Army. Even Washington's own officers whispered about replacing him.

The British now occupied New York City. They had declared the war over during the winter. The British officers were enjoying themselves, dining on the best food and wine and dancing minuets in ballrooms.

Christmas Eve found George Washington on the bank of the Delaware River. Ice flowed by on the swift current. Sleet stung his face. Winds snared his cape. His men had no shoes. They were hungry. The horses were shoeless, too. They slipped in the ice as they pulled wagons loaded with cannon to the riverbank. The British might have stopped fighting for the winter, but Washington saw this night as his last chance.

The British danced in ballrooms.

Washington's officers whispered about replacing him.

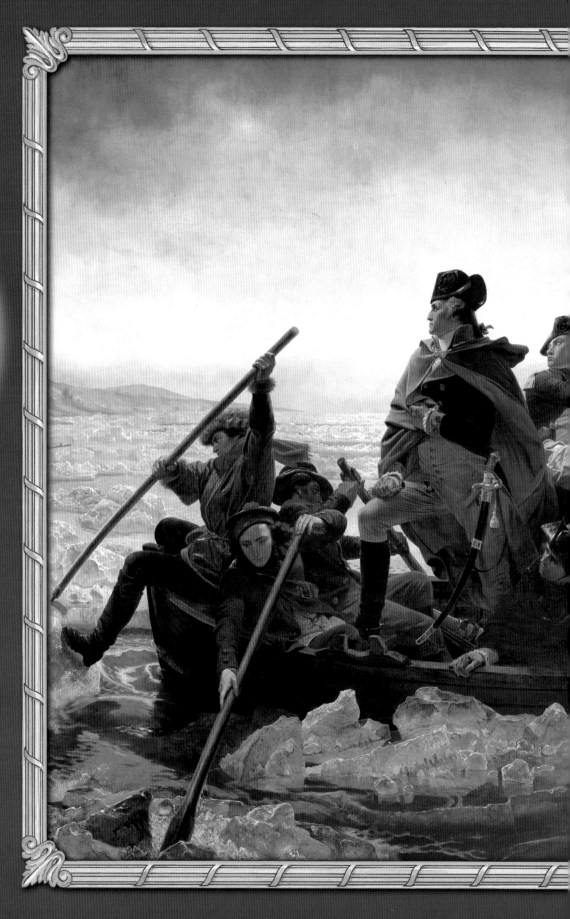

Across the river in Trenton, New Jersey, were Hessians (HESH-ens). They were soldiers from Germany, hired by King George to fight for England. If Washington could beat the Hessian troops, he might still win the war. If he failed, all might be lost forever. The mission's password showed how desperate Washington felt. It was "Liberty or Death."

The Hessian officers attended a Christmas celebration.

A spy in Washington's camp wrote a note to the Hessian general in Trenton, telling him that Washington planned to attack at dawn on Christmas day. But the Hessian general was attending a party. He did not want to be bothered. "They're half-naked," he said. "Let them come."

The Hessian general died in battle the next morning. In his pocket was the folded, forgotten note. Washington's desperate mission had succeeded.

When the British in New York City learned of General Washington's victory, their celebration came to an end. It seemed the war was not quite over yet.

That was exactly the message that Benjamin Franklin carried with him on board a ship bound for France. He was going to seek help from England's oldest and most hated rival. France had a powerful navy. France had money to feed and clothe and arm thousands of soldiers. Ben Franklin's mission was to convince France to join the fight.

Washington encouraged his weary, freezing, and hungry troops as they struggled across the Delaware River on Christmas Eve to surprise the Hessians.

The Turning Point

The king of France refused to see Ben Franklin. He believed England would easily beat the colonial army. Indeed, when a British force began to march south from Canada in 1777, most people believed the war would soon be over. The force was led by General John Burgoyne. His plan was to march to Albany, on the Hudson River in New York. If he captured it, he could cut off New England from the rest of the colonies. The march began well, but the British were in for a real surprise.

British Redcoats

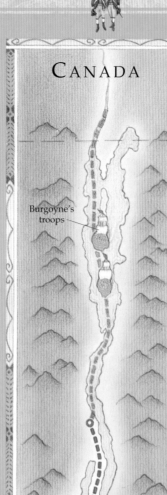

STRUGGLING

Long before Burgoyne's troops reached Albany, they were miserable. After four months on the road, they were nearly out of food. They had tried to capture horses and supplies, but they had failed. The discouraged men huddled around their campfires, exhausted.

① *Patriot sharpshooters perched in trees and fired down at the British soldiers, aiming first for the officers.*

FRIGHTENED

As British troops marched south, the Patriots fled. But they did not give up. They slowed the British march by chopping down trees to block the roads. They attacked unexpectedly from the woods. The British soldiers couldn't rest. And they became scared.

DISASTER

Just south of Saratoga, New York, the Patriots organized a force high above the road Burgoyne planned to take to Albany. Burgoyne could not march past them, so he ordered his men to fight. The fighting went very badly for the British. Finally, Burgoyne had to retreat, leaving seven hundred of his soldiers dead.

SCAVENGERS

British and Hessian camp followers slipped silently among the shadows on the battlefield at night, removing everything from the dead that could be used by the living—boots, pants, jackets, guns.

② *The British wore red coats to hide bloodstains. But they also made easy targets.*

General Burgoyne offered his sword in surrender.

SURRENDER

Burgoyne tried to turn around and march north, back toward Saratoga. The Patriots followed, and they "swarmed around the army like birds of prey," said one soldier. Finally General Burgoyne gave up. The Patriot rebels had beaten one of England's great generals, proving they could fight—and win. It was a turning point in the war.

To be sure the sight was truly astonishing... poor, dirty, starving men, great numbers of women and some very young, infants who were born on the road. Such an odor filled the air while they were passing. —Hannah Winthrop, 1777

MARCH OF DEFEAT

Patriot Hannah Winthrop saw the British and Hessian prisoners of war marching to a camp near Boston.

A WELCOME AT LAST

In France, the American victory at Saratoga was excellent news for Benjamin Franklin. The king of France agreed to enter the war.

Women at court crowned Ben Franklin with laurel leaves as an honor.

The World Turned Upside Down

By 1781, the war had been raging for six years. Even with France's help, the Patriots were struggling. They were losing important battles in the southern colonies. It seemed as if America's new flag of freedom would never fly. No one expected what happened next. On the York River in Virginia, not far from Felicity's home in Williamsburg, thousands of Patriot soldiers dug trenches around the village of Yorktown, where British troops were headquartered. The trenches protected the soldiers from British fire. The Patriots were preparing for what they thought would be a long and difficult battle.

TRAPPED!
British general Cornwallis wasn't worried by the Americans. He believed more British troops and ships were on their way. General Cornwallis did not know that the French navy had stopped the British ships and troops. By September, he and his troops were trapped in Yorktown, with no way to get food or supplies.

① *Cornwallis couldn't bring himself to surrender his sword. He sent a deputy to do it.*

SURRENDER
On the morning of October 17, American cannon were raining death on the British. By October 19, General Cornwallis had surrendered to General Washington. America had won its independence.

MARCH OF DEFEAT

The defeated British marched between
the Americans, laying down their
guns and burying their bayonets
point-first in the ground.

② *Washington, in return,
would not take the sword
from a deputy. He had a
deputy of his own accept it.*

IF BUTTERCUPS BUZZED

As they marched, the British army
musicians played a children's song
on their fifes and drums called
"The World Turned Upside Down."
The British regulars had been the
strongest army in the world. But
they had lost to the ragged American
rebels. For the British, the world
had indeed turned upside down.

STARS AND STRIPES

No one knows for
certain who sewed
the first American flag.
George Washington
might have asked Betsy
Ross of Philadelphia to
create a flag for the new
united colonies. America's
new flag had 13 stars, one
for each colony.

The World Turned Upside Down

If buttercups buzzed after the bee,
If boats were on Land, churches on sea,
If ponies rode men and grass ate the cows,
And cats should be chased to holes by the mouse,
If Summer were spring and t'other way round,
Then all the world would be upside down.

A Peek into the Future

"Thank you, Grandfather," Felicity said. "I promise to take good care of the guitar. Someday, when I am older, I'll play it for you. We'll sing together."

—Happy Birthday, Felicity!

At the start of the war, Felicity was ten years old. Before the war's end, she was a young woman of 16. What was her life like during those years of fighting? Perhaps she kept a diary, like so many of the American girls in this book. She might have "taken the pox" or received with great sorrow a letter sealed with black wax. She might have helped her mother pluck a goose. Surely she kept practicing her music lessons so she could entertain guests as a gentlewoman. Why, she might have even worn a headdress!

Like Eliza Lucas, she helped manage the Merrimans' store in her father's absence. At times during the fighting that raged all around her, she surely met soldiers—even British regulars.

Eliza Wilkinson, a Patriot in Charleston, South Carolina, kept a diary in which she wrote her feelings during the war: *A day of sorrow. I have seen my countrymen bound and dragged away. . . . We are entirely at the mercy of the British soldiers. Even women are sent to the prison ship.*

When a British soldier came to call, Eliza remained stiff but polite. After all, she was properly schooled as the daughter of a well-to-do family. When the soldier asked her to play her guitar for him, Eliza's answer was spirited.

"Not today. I won't play for you. Are you going to put me in prison?"

"When will you play again?" he asked.

"Not till my countrymen return . . . as conquerors!"

Felicity Merriman might have said something just like that.